FREAKY FISH

FANGTOOTH

BY KRISTEN RAJCZAK NELSON

 Gareth Stevens
PUBLISHING

Please visit our website, www.garethstevens.com. For a free color catalog of all our high-quality books, call toll free 1-800-542-2595 or fax 1-877-542-2596.

Cataloging-in-Publication Data

Names: Nelson, Kristen Rajczak.
Title: Fangtooth fish / Kristen Rajczak Nelson.
Description: New York : Gareth Stevens Publishing, 2018. | Series: Freaky fish | Includes index.
Identifiers: ISBN 9781538202647 (pbk.) | ISBN 9781538202586 (library bound) | ISBN 9781538202463 (6 pack)
Subjects: LCSH: Deep-sea animals–Juvenile literature. | Marine animals–Juvenile literature.
Classification: LCC QL125.5 N45 2018 | DDC 591.77–dc23

First Edition

Published in 2018 by
Gareth Stevens Publishing
111 East 14th Street, Suite 349
New York, NY 10003

Copyright © 2018 Gareth Stevens Publishing

Designer: Katelyn E. Reynolds
Editor: Joan Stoltman

Photo credits: Cover, pp. 1, 17, 21 (viperfish, lanternfish) Norbert Wu/Minden Pictures/Getty Images; cover, pp. 1–24 (background) Ensuper/Shutterstock.com; cover, pp. 1–24 (background) macro-vectors/Shutterstock.com; cover, pp. 1–24 (background) Kjpargeter/Shutterstock.com; cover, pp. 1–24 (fact box) nicemonkey/Shutterstock.com; p. 5 Mark Conlin/Oxford Scientific/Getty Images; p. 7 MARTYN HAYHOW/AFP/Getty Images; p. 9 GREGORY OCHOCKI/Science Source/Getty Images; p. 10 3DMI/Shutterstock.com; p. 11 ekler/Shutterstock.com; p. 13 Roland Birke/Photographer's Choice/Getty Images; p. 15 © President and Fellows of Harvard College/Museum of Comparative Zoology, Harvard University/CC BY-NC-SA 3.0; p. 19 David Shale/Nature Picture Library/Getty Images; p. 21 (six-gilled shark) Greg Amptman/Shutterstock.com; p. 21 (frilled shark) Awashima Marine Park/Getty Images; p. 21 (wolffish) © Citron/Wikipedia.org/CC-BY-SA-3.0.

Printed in the United States of America

CPSIA compliance information: Batch #CS17GS: For further information contact Gareth Stevens, New York, New York, at 1-800-542-2595.

CONTENTS

Words in the glossary appear in **bold** type the first time they are used in the text.

INTO THE DEEP

Deep at the bottom of the ocean is a whole world waiting to be discovered. In fact, much of it is still a mystery! We do know that the deep sea is home to one of the freakiest looking fish out there—the fangtooth fish!

This fish almost looks like a monster, but it can't hurt people. In fact, few people will ever even see one! It spends most of its life in water so deep, the sun doesn't even reach it.

FREAKY FACT!
The fangtooth fish is sometimes called the ogrefish because of its looks!

Would you find the fangtooth fish creepy if you came across it?

5

WHAT A GRIN!

The most recognizable feature of fangtooth fish is what they're named for—**fangs**! They have lots of huge, sharp teeth. These teeth look even scarier because fangtooth fish have small bodies with large heads and big mouths!

The fangtooth fish might look really creepy, but it's nothing to be afraid of. That's partly because of its size. The fangtooth fish is small! Most only grow to be about 6 to 7 inches (15 to 18 cm) long.

FREAKY FACT!

Fangtooth fish are covered in **scales** that are dark brown or black.

Like other fish, fangtooth fish have fins, the body parts that help fish swim. Their fins are on the top, bottom, and sides of their body.

SHUT YOUR MOUTH!

A fangtooth fish's fangs look a bit like the nails you might use to hang a picture. They're long and straight—and sharp!

The fangtooth fish has a cool **adaptation** so that it can close its mouth without hurting its head with its fangs. There are special holes in the fish's upper **jaw**. The sharp bottom teeth slide into the holes when the fish closes its mouth. The holes are found on either side of the fangtooth fish's brain!

FREAKY FACT!

When compared with the size of its body, the fangtooth fish has the largest teeth of any **marine** animal.

Without the special holes in its jaw, a fangtooth fish might bite too hard one day and stab its own brain! Freaky!

HOLE

Way Down Deep

Millions of fish swim in Earth's oceans, but the deeper you go, the fewer there are to see! The fangtooth fish is one of these rare deep-sea swimmers. Fangtooth fish are usually found 1,600 to 6,500 feet (500 to 2,000 m) deep. But they've been found as deep as 16,400 feet (5,000 m)!

The water is cold where fangtooth fish live, around 40°F (4°C) or a little warmer. Water turns to ice at 32°F (0°C), so their home is very cold!

Fangtooth fish are found in oceans all over the world except near Earth's poles.

Atlantic Ocean

Pacific Ocean

Pacific Ocean

Indian Ocean

fangtooth fish

PART OF THE PLANKTON

Fangtooth fish lay eggs. Between June and August, a female fangtooth fish will **release** her eggs into the water. Then, the male will swim over to **fertilize** them. After that, neither parent has anything to do with their babies again!

The larvae come out of their eggs and live much closer to the surface than adults do. Fangtooth fish larvae are part of the ocean's plankton, the tiny living things that float around in the water as they grow.

FREAKY FACT!
Female fangtooth fish are bigger than male fangtooth fish!

Along with the larvae of fangtooth fish, many other fish larvae live among ocean plankton!

LOOKING YOUNG

Until a young fangtooth fish is about 3 inches (8 cm) long, it looks very different from an adult fangtooth fish. Scientists used to think that young, or juvenile, fangtooth fish were a different species, or kind, of fangtooth fish!

Juvenile fangtooth fish have many different features than adults. They're lighter in color, and they have **spines.** They have very different teeth and fangs. In fact, juvenile fangtooth fish don't even live in the same depth of water as adults!

14

This young fangtooth fish may not have his big teeth yet, but he'll grow them soon enough!

On the Hunt

The fangtooth fish is a fierce deep-sea predator! Many fish that live in the deepest parts of the ocean are ambush predators, which means they wait for their **prey** to swim by and then grab it.

Not the fangtooth fish! Scientists believe fangtooth fish hunt for their food. They even swim closer to the surface at night to try to find a snack they'd like to chomp! Their scary teeth help to catch and kill prey.

FREAKY FACT!

Juvenile fangtooth fish eat mostly **crustaceans**. Adult fangtooth fish like fish and shrimp!

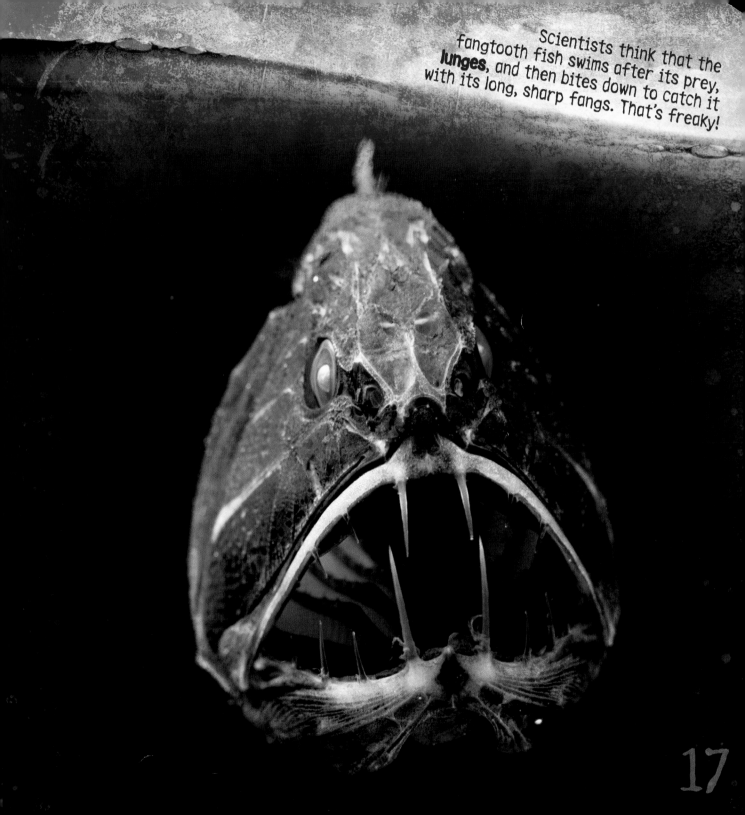

Scientists think that the fangtooth fish swims after its prey, **lunges**, and then bites down to catch it with its long, sharp fangs. That's freaky!

17

They Smell It Coming!

Because it's so dark where they live, fangtooth fish don't use their eyes to find their prey. They may look for their prey's shadow when even a little bit of sunlight has reached their depth in the ocean. But usually, they just use their sense of smell!

Even though fangtooth fish have such large teeth, they don't chew their prey. They swallow it whole! The fish they eat can be as much as one-third the size of the fangtooth fish.

FREAKY FACT!

Fangtooth fish are eaten by other fish, such as tuna and marlins.

Fangtooth fish's dark coloring blends in to the darkness of the deep ocean, keeping them hidden from both predators and prey.

MYSTERY FISH

There's still a lot scientists don't know about fangtooth fish! No one knows how many kinds of fangtooth fish there are. Little is known about their eggs and babies. Scientists don't even know how long fangtooth fish live!

We do know that their marine **ecosystem** must be kept healthy so that they can continue to live! If we do this, who knows what we'll learn about fangtooth fish! There's so much left to discover in the deep sea!

FREAKY FACT!

Scientist first discovered the fangtooth fish in the 1800s. It then took over 100 years before the next fangtooth fish discovery, a small fish called the shorthorn fangtooth!

OTHER FREAKY DEEP-SEA FISH

SIX-GILL SHARK
depth found: up to 8,200 feet (2,500 m)

FRILLED SHARK
depth found: up to 5,000 feet (1,520 m)

VIPERFISH
depth found: up to 13,000 feet (3,960 m)

WOLFFISH
depth found: up to 2,000 feet (610 m)

LANTERNFISH
depth found: up to 3,200 feet (975 m)

GLOSSARY

adaptation: a change in a type of animal that makes it better able to live in its surroundings

crustacean: an animal with a hard shell, jointed limbs, feelers, and no backbone, such as a shrimp or crab

ecosystem: all the living things in an area

fang: a long, pointed tooth

fertilize: to add male cells to a female's eggs to make babies

jaw: the bones that hold the teeth and make up the mouth

lunge: to suddenly move forward

marine: having to do with the sea

prey: an animal that is hunted by other animals for food

release: to set something free

scale: one of the flat plates that cover a fish's body

spine: one of many stiff, pointed parts growing from

FOR MORE INFORMATION

BOOKS

De la Bédoyère, Camilla. *Monsters of the Deep.* Richmond Hill, Ontario, Canada: Firefly Books, 2014.

Grady, Colin. *The Ocean Biome.* New York, NY: Enslow Publishing, 2017.

Lynette, Rachel. *Deep-Sea Anglerfish and Other Fearsome Fish.* Chicago, IL: Raintree, 2012.

WEBSITES

Deep-Sea Creatures
ocean.nationalgeographic.com/ocean/photos/deep-sea-creatures
Check out more freaky creatures that live deep underwater!

The Ocean's Weirdest Creatures!
ngkids.co.uk/animals/strange-sea-creatures#
Find more freaky ocean animals on this website!

INDEX